Between the Empty and the All

"across the schizophrenic gulf,
the acrobatic poet
tries on his brand new clothes"

~ Rod Deakin-Drown

Also by Rod Deakin-Drown

No Dog Barked : Who killed the Maclauchlans?
Rod Drown & Ken McIntosh.
(Archives New West Publishing 2018)

The New Westminster Frasers Baseball Club
Rod Drown & Ken McIntosh (2010)
2010

Early Logging Methods in the Golden Area.
Rod Drown
(Golden and District Historical Society 1994)

Between
the Empty
and
the All

by

Rod Deakin-Drown

720 – Sixth Street, Box # 5
New Westminster, BC
V3C 3C5   CANADA

Title: Between the Empty and the All
Author: Rod Deakin-Drown
Publisher: Silver Bow Publishing
Cover Art: "Nightfall" 2018 painting by Candice James
Editing: Candice James

All rights reserved including the right to reproduce or translate this book or any portions thereof, in any form without the permission of the publisher. Except for the use of short passages for review purposes, no part of this book may be reproduced, in part or in whole, or transmitted in any form or by any means, electronically or mechanically, including photocopying, recording, or any information or storage retrieval system without prior permission in writing from the publisher or a licence from the Canadian Copyright Collective Agency (Access Copyright).

www.silverbowpublishing.com
info@silverbowpublishing.com
© Silver Bow Publishing 2019

Library and Archives Canada Cataloguing in Publication

Title: Between the empty and the all / by Rod Deakin-Drown.
Names: Deakin-Drown, Rod, 1948- author.
Description: Poems.
Identifiers: Canadiana (print) 20190136103 | Canadiana (ebook) 20190136111 | ISBN 9781774030547
   (softcover) | ISBN 9781774030554 (HTML)
Classification: LCC PS8607.E237 B48 2019 | DDC C811/.6—dc23

Dedication

To Isabelle, my lovely wife
and Warrior of the Western Heart

And

To Wendy, long-time friend
and Champion of the Poetic Art.

Between the Empty and the All

FOREWORD
~ by Wendy Watson, B.A. English; (PDP), Simon Fraser University.

When Rod asked me to write a forward to this collection, I was reticent: literary analysis had not been my post secondary academic career. Therefore, I decided to "write what I know": the themes, passions, and life struggles behind some of the works chosen for this collection.

Let's begin with the book's title poem, "Between the Empty and the All". My first response was tears. I was led quickly on a first read from playful young soldiers in France, to the slaughter of Flanders, to a ghost story of *"the honoured, the bitterly wasted dead"*. In this poem Rod has fused universal and family loss: Rod's great uncle Ted experienced the horrors of Flanders. Like many men of his era, Rod's great uncle did not talk of the horror. But, says Rod, Ted did retain the playful humor of the young soldiers who *"grabbed the girls"* and *"told them jokes and little lies"*.

I love "Cane, Top Hat and Tails" because it evokes, for me, the image of Rod, over the years, arriving at my door, unannounced, dressed dramatically in clothing reflecting his evolving poetic personae and growing sense of self and of wit. His entrances were always accompanied by a unique flourish: - *"The acrobatic poet tries on his brand new clothes."*

A widow's pain in the poem *"Cedar Ends the Century"*, recalls a tragic 1950's accident in Rod's hometown of Golden, BC, where a man was crushed under cedar posts in a wintertime accident. It is followed by two others that also reflect personal loss and iconic moments: "Fifteen Years Ago" and "Dislocation" which were inspired by the passing of Rod's father, who lost his life in a farming accident.

"We were all captured, engraved / by nightmares of tractors / falling over banks; / by reveries and memories of last moments /as our cosmos dislocated itself."

In poetry, as in Rod's life, women are treated with profound respect. A newer poem, "Let Me Be Your Lancelot", one of many "courtly love" examples in this collection, introduces the love of Rod's life, Isabelle.

"So gather the sun in your sky-blue dress / and wear the fields of green in your hat / As you and Percival ride / along the shady forest track / I am beside you too - / in spirit, idea, and thought / Let me be your Lancelot".

My favourite ending lines in this collection are from, "I Fall to Earth" , inspired by Isabelle's tripping mishap in Paris and her description of it in English, "I fall to earth":

"Your soul, my soul's friend / You, my best guarantee against unhappy endings".

Contents

Saltant Sexuality ... 13
Cottonwood Planet ... 14
Notes from the Balmoral ... 16
Daggers, Words and Beautiful Nets ... 17
Skye's World ... 18
Mile 147, Alaska Highway ... 19
Mary-Janed ... 20
Cedar Ends the Century ... 22
Zhivago's Alley ... 23
Raking Leaves ... 25
Empire Unrecognized ... 26
Shaking Off Boulders ... 27
Disguises ... 28
Wisdom, Knowledge and Grimaces While Stuttering ... 30
October Glade ... 31
Dreams ... 32
Bus Depot Scene ... 33
Young Summertime Girl ... 34
Cane Top Hat and Tails ... 35
Synchronicity ... 36
Indians ... 37
Between the Empty and the All ... 38
Our Shadows Never Sleep ... 39
Coast ... 40
On the Ridge Trail ... 41
Salt Spring Suite ... 42
Flares the Sun ... 43
I Dreamed a Summer of My Childhood ... 44
Buried Dusty Box ... 45
Winter's Water to the Truck ... 46
Melancholy ... 47
Cathedral ... 48

Letting in Light ... 49
Dragonflies ... 50
Contemplation ... 51
I Will Not Be Like That ... 52
Leaving Shelter Bay ... 51
Poem for Tatiana ... 54
Kisses in Victoria Station ... 55
Inside Dreamed Outside ... 57
Off the Diving Board ... 58
Windowed Clocks ... 59
You Are Loud in My Skin ... 60
Allison Fenn ... 61
At the Edge of the Sea ... 62
Coming Home One Day ... 63
A Poem for Juliana ... 64
Joyce's Room ... 65
Time to Go ... 66
Alchemy ... 67
Until Your Next Roaming ... 68
Mirrors ... 69
Riding with Susan ... 70
Icarus' Dream ... 72
This Morning Table ... 73
My Bed Will Hold Us Nicely ... 75
Spires, Signals, Sky ... 76
This Is Our River ... 77
Sailing ... 78
The Stutterer's Kiss ... 79
Summer's Dance ... 80
These Rooms of Yours ... 81
Light ... 82
So Many Lifetimes with You ... 83
Quiet Astonishment ... 84
Secret House ... 85
I Float into Sleep's River ... 86

The Long Arc ... 87
This Much Is True ... 89
Darker Powers ... 91
Fifteen Years Ago ... 92
Dislocation ... 93
Let Me Be Your Lancelot ... 94
Isabelle ... 95
I Fall to Earth ... 96
History's Untraceable Pedestrians ... 97

Between the Empty and the All

Saltant Sexuality

afternoons
we are linked by sunshine
the ice melts,
mornings
a fog comes almost to our knees
and we are people moving on mist

natural children
of Terpsichore

let us quick-pull our love!
let me glide into you
we must slide
leaving
  learning
spurning
then twining
coming back together again

Cottonwood Planet

The sea is grey, all equators crazy
a mane vast and unreported
liquid slate before the dawn
but the tides move, spray of a great heart beating
a blood drop of chlorophyll green
by its sun by the black
and its silk water trembling,

the earth and me carried,
I and breathing and a farmer's lane.
Here poplars tower aflame in shimmer
a silver surface green, not silver at all

I parted grasses
under jet trails evenly dying
in the stratospheric winds above
great white clouds in the sky,
they rose an avalanche jumbled high
over the new mountains
over my heart's remembered world
old fields though grown full
I had deserted
I revisited

I lunged slow leap through all
that keeps becoming the ruins
in the lives of soldiers' wives
that they aimed for
told and defamed for buying
glasses in the local legion hall.

heartbeat and kiss and too much green
life's spirit subsided then burst
from the green earth,
sun hidden all

Between the Empty and the All

my feet on the gravel road
I came to be thirteen years old
my blindness mended
the ceilings of Heaven descended, unending.

I wanted to climb trees and clouds,
like an ant-foot dangler
on bark finger-cliffed,
its granite flexed, me stiff but bending.
I drifted through our summer fields
to there – the ceiling centred,
that tree where the sheep grazed
and rolled in its shade forty years ago,
the exact black-white mirror of old photographs.

Notes from the Balmoral 1:
Police passing through at Indian hour

Vancouver's dark blue Rhinoceros chorus line,
shoulder-swims, tough stomach-swings
its way through the bar,

movie: John Law in the raw.

Notes from the Balmoral 2:
Beer Bringer, Prime Kind

It's young Groucho Marx in an ivory shirt.
sharp-shadowed clear beer waiter,
blue-eyed alert.
moustache smile all through the bar

Daggers, Words and Beautiful Nets

There is no safety
when the crowd
is numbered in flatterers

There is little time to bide
when clowning assassins
flock like peacocks to your side

Skye's World

faces flushed, shadows stark
some smiles tight
a photographer flashed us
in the sun and wind,
not in the trout-scale ivory shine
of soft estival moonlight

that's me reading to your father
I – the young saint gone intellectual
he the reverend gone bad

that's you – blonde angel in the corner
like a breeze, almost whispering
the spiritual world ain't half so bad

Mile 147, Alaska Highway

Beautiful in August
My dear young woman kneeled
on a tall sunlit stump
in half a red bathing suit.

love, naked waist up
you had the most beautiful breasts
I had ever seen.

feeling good on *imported* wine
eating cheese and French bread
you were trying to lure boy virgins
and seduce
their rich old grandfathers.

Irish Lady
flirting wench
I see you now and I feel how
I will rise to long leather lengths
to keep you.

I want to reach you from here
from the rolling damp dark muskeg
below a star-scattered calabas sky
I will drift and scheme
walking scrape-top across the spruce forest
along the sky
from diamond to diamond
and down a glittering cosmic road
to plan our dreams
standing on hill tops
going wild in South America
planning nothing
but slipping away to Buenos Aires.

Mary-Janed

I lay there beside you
you that kept changing
you quick, the chameleon
of my perceived reactions,
intentions and our mutual situations.

Like a photograph beside a stream,
I lay there beside you
counting daisies off my pillow
that turned into butterflies.

Like a painter chained before the seasons,
I lay there beside you,
you that kept changing
and saw great metaphysic
warp holes that I would fall into
and come out of twisted
if I came out at all

Like a blueprint man in unscripted form
torn, racing from logic to logic
finally getting lost
in process and realizing
that, yes, I was moving so fast
that I was static
and infinite
and that it was so autumnally nice
to find something to lean on,
that would allow me
to build a church out of you.

I made my plans, I set my scene
Like shadows lost and wanting dreams
I decided on love
I decided I would

Between the Empty and the All

heed all the signposts
of your actions and words
and careen around them accordingly.

Midnight water woman,
Do you know you sleep
at ten thousand miles an hour?

Cedar Ends the Century

a pioneer
up on the winter hill
steep above the swamps
hauling down the fast slippery track
in the white noon of December

horses hitched by double tree
the sled braked
and weighted by cedar

hauling down seven foot posts
for around the coming summer's hay crop
in the snow's opaque shade.
through heavy cloud
sun seen like a moon
low on the horizon

Charlie was, my father said,
as old as the year.
meeting fear
on the winter hill

lost control
on the slippery snow
overturning the sled
he was a long time dying
under the cedar scent.

pioneer wife shed a tear
overcome by the smell of cedar

Zhivago's Alley

I woke up from a dream,
in which I had laid beside
God's most divine light,
to the sounds of freight trains
rumbling through the night.

A river of steel on rails
passing down the valley
carried its sound to my bed
like a wedding of two houses:
one steel and dreaded
the other wood and Holy leaf.

Did you know that parts
of Dr. Zhivago were filmed here,
that these mountains were the Urals,
a revolutionary world?

Columbia River, and its valley
Zhivago's alley, Zhivago's valley.
I look for Lara everywhere

So let me say to Thee of Thy Beauty:
It is inner *and* outer
joy, gentle heart and loveliness
below and above.

If I were Zhivago;
If I were lost in a storm
rounding some desolate private Cape Horn
on a wintry sea
without hope of being saved;
and if I had loved Thee but once
that once would last me
through all hard times engraved.

Between the Empty and the All

If I were Zhivago;
if I were lost in a storm and
if I had loved Thee but twice,
the time between the first and last
would have been harder than the hardest wave.

If I were Zhivago;
if I were lost in a storm and
if I had loved Thee but thrice,
I'd light up the candles, melt the ice from the masts!
I would be by Thy side, though the sea with fire be paved.

Such beauty as yours,
in and out,
saves men like me from caves of sorrow.

Raking Leaves

Things are always sad in raking leaves
last summer's beauties from last summer's trees

I sat in front of the house
and looked at the garden you built
under the steps.
I have let it all go to waste

The tarpaper is all dirty and torn
and the wood chips you placed there,
caring for how things looked,
have all slid down. What am I to do?
Now that I don't have you
and never will again.

Here, why am I alone
on a Sunday afternoon
between the hammer and the stone?

You loved me as you saw me.
Why am I born this way,
every lifetime a key slightly awry
and rusty from before,
from tears all at the core of things?

I sat in front of the house
and looked at the gardens
you had tried to build.

Now I remember every woman
who ever loved me
who in the end
her affection I killed.

Empire Unrecognized

I am an empire unrecognized

I am a bridge full of sighs
I have a cathedral inside my throat.

There is a room without a door
But a sky that seeks a floor
I have a melody and need the notes.

I sleep in a small high ceiling room
Where brides' souls seek Solar grooms
My song is a full moon boat

I am a Christ a-slowly born
Once a scarecrow among the corn
My voice between the birds' afloat.

Shaking off Boulders

Lips on lips, sipping slipping worlds
the words escaping like creeks, streaming
through boulders and ice jams,

to hymns swinging black as soul,
coal to diamond, diamonds by ice
melting in glaciers riddled through
with cathedral blue caves
where I wander in trusting, thrusting awe.

Disguises

Do not be alarmed
We lead charmed lives.

I shall wear disguises, some disquieting
others wise or foolish

I shall stride the streets at dusk or dawn
bearded, not bearded, glasses off or slouch hat on

You will run for buses in snowstorms
Come, evenings, out of nowhere

Do not be alarmed.
We lead charmed lives.

I shall be timely seen at certain corners or,
unexpectedly serene,

exiting certain basement doors
reported to have been with card players, torrid women
or light-fingered perfumed connoisseurs.

You will drift through Central Europe,
not apologetic, writing papers not yet poetic.

Do not be alarmed.
We lead charmed lives.

I shall be there in a dozen different ways,
catching your straying glances as, in
a passing bus, you chance to look.

I will be the bookseller, the Watchtower teller
the hot dog guy by the steel buffalo
the panhandler quiet by stealth

Between the Empty and the All

or bent down by dwindling health
shaking in a winter wind,
some disguises clichés and catch phrases.

Still I will enchant, surprise.
Concede defeat, rise again,
deny all expectations.

Do not be alarmed
We lead charmed lives.

At bus stops, lonely docks,
near-deserted morning sidewalks
you will be converted by what connects.

Still, nothing will be proven, 'til you,
asunder under a starry, starry night,
look me in the eye, then get us right.

I think of you sideways leaning
head against the window
of the bus, your resting folded hands

in your lap, weary enough to
drift astray to former days
in Moldova, Rumania, Israel.

I think I once was blind.
Long coat and white cane dangling,
everything inside-out. Doubt

everything *but the heart*.
Part with self-inflicted camouflage:
Deny not the deluge, the rainbow, the mirage.

Wisdom, Knowledge, and Grimaces While Stuttering

Wisdom , knowledge,
and grimaces while stuttering

while stuttering hideously
am I trying to hide my facts?
Hide facts and feelings
forehead knit like a map
of anger, sorrow, pain
an intense clown's world
of bizarre refrains.

Say Shadow breaking through
Or trying to
Time trying to catch up
See the clock hid beneath my face and forehead
Or almost hid
Almost and sometimes entirely hidden
But always hideous in the attempt.

Poor Shadow
So few places to go
So few places I can take you
Take my hand and let us go together
You are the tattered feather in my cap.

The weathered feather of all my strivings
And complicated arrivings

October Glade

our life slows
the morning flows calmly
we breathe
like we are in separate rooms

the room is a clutter
of paintings and etchings
old socks and discarded underwear

our closet is full
of your previous life's shoes
and my old newspapers

the clock ticks
and I

in the orange Mexican housecoat that was yours
the one with the "GI" overtones
(you -- exotic sparring champion of old Mexico
me – the best lay north of the Rio Grande)
sit at my desk
and write poetry
about you fallow in bed
on a late ten-thirty morning
dreaming of brilliant valleys to the green seashore
and little people swimming in turquoise pools.

we are champions
confined
to bed and pen.

Dreams

You want to be perfect
But the perfect spheres go rolling by
As the cloud cities fade into sky

Oh, ma, there was a glimpse
that was so fine
There was a diamond tear
from my golden eye

There was a lady with silver heels
and smooth fine lines,
There were nights in castles
with mystic gypsy girls
who danced on quiet fire

Oh, ma, there was a glimpse
that was so fine,
There was a mansion
where the beggars dine,
There was a lady with silver heels
with ankles smooth and fine beauty lines.

Will there be another chance?
A second vision on the Joker's grace?
Will the dragon come by again?
Will I drag the visor down my face
stumble to my horse outside,
take my heroic sword and ride?

Bus Depot Scene

omniscient but still suspicious
old ladies
give disapproving catatonic eye
like jealous birds paralyzed
by irritation
to those young men
with strong young women
passing through, sweet and lithe,
on the road from youth
to loss of expectation.

Young Summertime Girl,

Evenings, I have watched you descend the
buses, and slip down tree-lined
star-shadowed streets
sweeping leaves with your feet

I once caught you young
and strong in June
summer job-hunting in a brand-new dress
fresh as the new green grass
twice as much alive

Cane, Top-Hat and Tails

there are revealing things
a man cannot
discuss or disclose.
so with an evasive leap
across the schizophrenic gulf,
the acrobatic poet
tries on his brand new clothes

Synchronicity

The Hastings Express rattles me across the bridge.
Halfway along I get off for pie and tea
then, there, up the larynx of my eye slides
one lurching drunk held together by safety pins and gin.
He rises unsteadily in the Aristocratic Café
at Broadway and Granville
and flashes a loose-lipped, too pink face
into one fleeting second of my awkwardness
and my mind's geography creases new shapes
in the rush of his smash-faced surprise:
it is an interrupted dancer's rise to anorexic suicide,
a beautiful thug-soldier's prance
along the shit-filled, bullet-pilled trenches,
a few seconds young and strong
then gone like the cat on the fence
or the bird bloody on the grassy ground,
all share the eagle's surprise in lack of sound
all are the round limp face, sickly soft
smashing into my eye like a wasp
in a telescoping café
while ten minutes away
sits Marianne by her sand paintings.

Indians

I came to an island
that was on fire
I searched for
and found a night of a full moon
and the water spark surface flowing
like a diamond snake moving into the bay
opaque size of dog's eyes
campfire bright,
Indians,
their old bones beneath the grass
their spirits are all in the trees now
their rustling shadows say
they made love violently
in complete campsite despair.

Between the Empty and the All

Oh they grabbed the girls
told them jokes and little lies,
those young Flanders' soldiers
with firm set mouths
and determined eyes
are now shadows in empty houses
existing in dim lit psychic intersections
where angels fear to tread
lest they wake the honoured,
the bitterly wasted dead
who are only dreams now,
vague as smoke

who exist below the castle and its wall
outside the bedroom in the hall,
lost,
between the empty and the all.

Our Shadows Never Sleep

Our shadows do not leap
from figure to figure
They lie sun struck
across lively bodies in flight
And slip moonstruck
across darker figures at night

Our shadows never sleep

They travel from room to room
yard to yard
house to house

We are not so brave as our shadows
They do not care who they lie with

Coast

evening ends.
the horizons around
are sharp and sheer

In the absence of a sail-thin moon
I feel safe here,
encircled and sealed
to the pale candle of your flesh
like a flame
found strong in an astral place
where there is no wind
and no moon
but stars everywhere
affecting.

Your woman's body is full
with the lunar calm
of ancient ocean strength.

On the Ridge Trail

On the ridge trail
where winter whipped the poplars yearly
up through the forest
cracked the tangle, cut between
listened to birds unseen,
mysterious distant whistles pagan
from the green layer subterranean
to the quick hot breeze in which they flew,
drifting and nimble to the sky.

Salt Spring Suite

the sun, the foam, the granite ladder
downward.

We traded the wine,
I knew your limbs with kisses

your dress was a wisp of white temptation
our trees controlled; the gulls patrolled
that wind which rode the sunrise

your spirit, and I
then restful with you between the rocks
and the sprayed weather-beaten cliffs,

naked and young, we
naked and strong

so proud of our youth
so full of the sun.

Flares the Sun

Flares the sun
alive deep in blue deep above
the summer Selkirks sloping west,
the fields of thick-legged Hereford cattle
at cud in green farms beneath
the Rockies' heaved-up granite wall
of forest, then steep red cliff,
lit shifting by the sun's setting
across the valley.

my sun
our sun,
love and life-long distance deep
one with the grass, the trees
and the crows free flying.

I Dreamed a Summer of My Childhood

I dreamed of being back on the farm;
the sun was setting
where the horizon hollowed down
along the northern ends of ridges,
where the river's bend descending
curled south to the valley of the Columbia
and went round the Selkirk Mountains.

I dreamed a summer of my childhood;
I was waiting for my parents
as dusk's shadow roiled itself
from the pine tree aisles,
down the hillside gullies beyond and behind
the age-powdered logs and grey shingle roofs
of the old henhouse and the big hayshed.

and then I dreamed I was awake
dreaming inside the dream.

Buried Dusty Box

Your past, buried
in a dusty box
with locks that ache like teeth.

Its shadows snag your fragility
even beside sand-edged oceans
rippling beneath summer's bluebird skies.

Oceans of tears drain
from your buried dusty box
and leave wave marks stained
not just on your sad face
but on all those
whose names
broke your trust
like smallpox.

Winter's Water to the Truck

Through the jack pine forest
I pack water, two pails a trip.
Shoulders straight tight grip.
Hands, wrists – weight stretching.

On this daily winter trip
to the frozen river I think
of your hands and wrists;
how you say they ache.

I think of your life;
the weights you carry.
The burdens you lift
as, from your dreams,
the past dangles
and draws your fingers
like angry anchors
through the flesh
of your arms and legs.

They have steel claws,
these ancient ravens
on your shoulders.
I imagine their weight
and try for your sake
to make them birds of paradise
singing now like nightingales.

Melancholy

Now you start to ask me
about our relationship:
Where is it going
and what is it for?
As if you don't believe
in my rainbows anymore.
At such questions, my blood
floods cold from beneath
where I hold my bated breath.
And I begin yet again:
to behold the *dismal*
within the *might-be-broken*.

I have an invisibly choking bride
on my hands and melancholy
enters the air, announcing pain
like a distant sickness coming:
there's a drummer in the shadows,
he's drumming summer's dusk
for all the leaves that fall.

Cathedral

I have a cathedral caught in my throat.
Its spires, rising, spike my heart.
Our telephone lines bend in its silence.

I have a cathedral caught in my throat.
There are hymns arising from confusion.
The singers wait for the old reunion.

Sometimes the voices are very soft
as when we have an ancient choir lost
in the memories of what I came here to do
with the fields, their presently broken fences
and the hayshed roofs with the loosened tin
lifted by October winds bringing down the leaves
that crumble on the ground by river-drift
the golden sunset cliffs, the hard grey rocks
of Mount Red Indian.

Still, I have a cathedral caught in my throat.
And you, choking on this life, have found one too.

Letting in Light

I dreamed of you last night

we were sweeping out rooms
and letting in light.

I threw out my old broken case
and brought down the cocoons
hanging from the ceiling.

Put some out for time and tide
all for the ancient fire
and me beside it, kneeling.

There are broken poems everywhere.
I will gather them up,
for the old fisherman reeling.

He will put them all together,
the laughter to the light,
all my words to their feelings.

Dragonflies

I like dragonflies you said
at one point
as I lived at the tips of your fingers
and in the straight goods of your smile.

I like dragon flies you said
as I moved, a story in your hands,
matching your guilelessness.

I like dragonflies you said
running your caress along my body
summoning the dragon of my being.

Even after
I still wondered about your eyes,
your smile and your dragonflies

How wonderful to meet a woman,
wise enough to know
when to bring her Goddess in
and then to sing
her dragonflies and her childhood.

Contemplation

Here, the Blaeberry
flowing by
and I in contemplation

of you
by the Cam
a third the world away,
the far side
of an ocean
full of hours.

Contemplation
of you
licking the stamp
as I dialed the number.

The universe falls free
to Thee and me

in Heavenly
Eros.

I Will Not Be Like That

Leave to other men their little lives
their suits and ties
rags and bones
sticks and stones,
all the places in their hearts unknown.

I will not be like that.
I will wear my own true hat
my coat of brighter colours.

Leave to other men
their politics
of defining clause,
endless petty difficulty
where obvious agendas
sent saints to endless boredom.

I will not be like that.
I will wear my own true hat
Infinite dreams of hilltop women lovers.

No, I will not be like that.
I will bear my own true candle
among the lamps at Johnson's Landing.

Leaving Shelter Bay

The ship of my life sets sail
Under the broken veil of clouds
That covers Arrow Lake,
Her valley and her mountains.

The ferry's tremble
Matches that in my soul
As I consider this control
I have lost in the oceans
I see within your eyes.

I want no one else but you
I want nothing but my Laurel lives.

Poem for Tatiana

Send me poems of who you are
The stars your packsack contains.

Send me your Mona Lisa smile
The treasures your hands have held.
Tell me the things you would not sell.
And I will give you mine:
Morning bells and evening seashells
No blinding diamond rings to bind!

Send me your suitcases of light
from the train trips of your dreams
Sail the waves and rain swept skies
Leave with me; leave all else behind.

Meet me late in a small cafe
Or seaside shelter in the rain.

But send me poems of who you are
The stars your packsack contains.

Kisses in Victoria Station

It is coming summer
here at Riverview.

The lawns fill my window
with their breadth and breath;
But you are gone, gone, gone.

Blue sky fails to distant bays of cloud.
Your picture punctuates my wall
in this strange land's little room
where I have ended up
being not too much at all.

Back there, fair:
You're on my knee
smiling your straight goods smile

At a breakfast time
of cheese, oranges
and caresses sweet and fresh as cucumbers.

Here, I gaze upon the grounds
as patients, some vague and old,
stroll the pathways to Pennington Hall.

More than 12 years ago
you went to Cambridge
and last year, a January day,
you died on a Cambridge Highway.

I loved you deep and strong
though winters cold and summers long.
Remember how we got there?
Remember your trip with me
across England, Wales and Dreamland.

Between the Empty and the All

I miss your goodbye kisses in Victoria Station.
Miss that sweet saxophone situation
gracing the bottom of the escalator.
Miss your whisper, every kiss's reason,
Miss each design for all our coming seasons.

Inside Dreamed Outside

Inside dreamed outside
Cave dreamed land and sky
Narrow dreamed wide
Wave dreamed, wending, why

Inmates, bars, drained from jails
Beds emptied of fairy tales
Trains above their rails
Minds, just enough details

This is the gate swinging
The golden bells ringing
Bringing in the Dawn
The key just within reach
The untouched beach

We in our boat
Coasting to shore.
More does not exist.

Off the Diving Board

Off the diving board
I am.

Above the clouds
and ghosts
of your foreign land.

In the place
of your face and sky.

Where our myths unforgotten
leave you unforgettable
and me seeking.

Windowed Clocks

Windowed clocks on many dressers
and outside ...

curved golden swords
summarize comma'd skies
slow diving into dusk
over deep green streets
of trees,
darkening lagoons, leaves
below obsidian horizons
behind obscure houses
on obscure streets;
shadows curled around light

and inside ...
windowed clocks on many dressers

You Are Loud in My Skin

Golden wheat fields wave the wind
signaling
Heaven's brim blue sky,

You are loud in my skin,
sap in my veins,
my airplane's wing, my clarinet singing.

Tip of my tongue,
I await.
grace from your mouth

Allison Fenn

She is Nightingale quiet
and straight framed and caring,
unruffled and from a deep quiet inside,
walks lightly the night-time hallways.

She looks in on the ladder-men
who, climbing their way to join the Moon's far side,
live above stream-sides missing from rooms
of unrequited loneliness.

At the Edge of the Sea

Where, last night, my wings used to be
replaced with ache of missing you
I have grown new control
as the sun rolls
steady slow
distant shimmering circle aflame
etched in silver gold.

New day:

in which I will drive
you and I to the seashore
in a deep blue Jaguar car
and feed you chocolates
shaped like diamonds
under a new blue sky;
and give you silk's refined
delicate butterfly wings;
and two lions at our wrists
as the mists lift to grandeur and distance.

How you make me weak;
then strong in my longing,
Tani-woman.

Coming Home One Day

Coming home one day
I saw you again
Like in a church, still

I just looked away

Coming home one day
I saw you on the train
Your face in a circle

My hopes down the drain

You said on the phone
You just didn't care
But I still see your face

Every place, everywhere

On the train alone
You, me, connecting day
You cast the briefest smile

I remembered Craig's Café

A Poem for Juliana

today
there are noises –like weed whackers
cracking apart my world
of morning poetic silences.

other times, ,
there are melodic voices with stories
and lovers' syllables willing eternity
from ecstasy's dreams and perfect flesh.

In a late night's dayroom lounge
our voices crept round memories
from former cities, pities and years
and we exchanged tales of
how hard it is escaping regrets.

For though we are people who have chosen
Life over Death –
a sailing moon over a belt,
a swoon over endless gloom,
we are still always somewhat broken
in this chaotic room of lives
only partly spoken.

I am glad you chose life.
For though I am not your lover
I would sit with you
in a subtle wind
on a sandy beach,
and wait upon a sailing moon,
to breeze through a sky
of whispering pale twilight,
and wish you well, always.

Joyce's Room

She is usually quiet at her work.
Her fingers are messengers.
Her caresses are blessings.

Joyce's room has secrets.
All pleasures there
come with regrets.

She is the Shadow Goddess
tending the fire of the flesh

Time to Go

It is but a walk out the door
and then gone for evermore

It is but a walk across the lawn
And soon the world we know is gone

All this anger, all this rage
Standing on a broken stage

Break the chains, pick up the reins
Leave this world of pale ink stains

Draw the curtains, end the show
Walk with me. It's time to go.

Alchemy

I dream of a trail marked Number 8
and two whippet dogs with me
as we climb toward
a snow-covered peak in Greece

I dream in a bed, a basement suite
sweet cocoon, red ochre room

Down the hill in the night
the Fraser flows past moorings
of fishing boats below the towers
in the shadow of the volcano
to the south with snow.

Until Your Next Roaming

Wandering Moldavian,
immigrant Angel,
let me be your home
until your next roaming.

I have been utterly true to you
without guile, true as an arrow
borrowed from God.

Let us borrow freely
from each other.

Let us laugh from towers,
sing songs through walls,
toss clocks through hours.

And I will suffer when you go.

Your boat will come,
white sail sunk low
on the horizon
and out of sight.

Day and night.
Body, soul.
Shade...then light.

Let me be your home
until your next roaming,
Tatiana delightful.

Mirrors

The redheaded girl stood in the doorway
when I was insane with the dawn behind her

deep blue apple tree infected dawn behind her,
her name forgotten
locked away in a clockwork trunk
a cascade of birthday cakes locked away
red-haired Allison

I awoke nine years old
as she crossed the threshold
to join her parents in the car
a wagon train to eternity
school, high school, college, lodge

Some perfect mornings once:
dreamt leaving Heaven together,
waking ache-less

Near-perfect nooks by noon;
hayfields glow soft, more green than hymns
fesque, timothy, alfalfa, lavender
under sky hanging blue to bursting
then decay: waning, late in the day,
dangled to dimness, thin as a scarecrow
left out in the rain.

Through staccato serenades
and broken parades
a veil of tears lifted
in the distance

became mirrors
to sleep in
to dream.

Riding with Susan

From the furthest star away
in the God-sprayed glitter scatter
of the Milky Way
to the after-shift drive
along the Fraser River
after work in your babe blue car;

From my most distant
memory of a playmate
lost after a six year old's summer
of hide and seek
below split-the-sky granite peak
on the farm;

to your smile, your wise eyes
your stories of Alzheimer's patients
lost in their fading footstep places
and retreating traces of memories.

Every drive home was unforgettable.

I am six years old again
in how I miss you.

I saw your wrist in a daylight dream,
in purple flowered jewelry,
with streaks of violet halos
in stones of amber, and azure.

There is a sky everywhere
full of seasons, reasons for regret;
springs for hope,
winters for discontent,
sunsets of legendary days
over bays filled with sailboats

Between the Empty and the All

quirky in the wind
and hillside-howling lonely wolves

seeking to begin,
and begin again.

Icarus' Dream

Where the rocks
are far below

and the sky
has no end,

I have been
with magnificence.

I know the sun.
Its bursting light
guides me.

There my body
glides, soars
to the silent roar
of the blonde ocean;

Yellow, the heat.
I was crazy with desire
for the sun
as it warmed the ocean below
and moved the old glaciers
slowly.

This Morning Table

I have just emerged from two dreams,
one merely an elaboration of another,
its deeper, wiser sister-brother.

At the end of the first
I remember sitting at my midnight table
writing of eternity
and the eternal apple tree
that stands forever in my veins,
and of your eternal beauty,
the one beneath the pleasant stain
of your youth's fleeting moment.

At the end of the second
I sat on a bus
seeing a dark-haired young woman
yelling fuck me fuck me
all you want to do is fuck me.

You were on that bus,
an angel full of grace,
tired, across the aisle sleeping.

A reflection, I suppose
of my soul's weariness,
its ache from movement creeping.

I sit at this morning table
considering the too short silence
this universe now is able to maintain
from mountain top to glacier
on this small blue marble
that floats uneasily
in the moat of a light-scattered blackness.

Between the Empty and the All

I sit at this morning table,
considering your hand's trace
on my shoulder,
the scene between
the coming rage of snow machines,
and not my resignation,
but my quiet wiser contemplation
of your eyes, your smile,
your touch retained
your very being
as it appears to me.
Sweet as Tupelo Honey
but fragile
in your present lingering illness.

Fragile
as our grasp of eternity.
You are
one of my everlasting memories,
dear Lee.

My Bed Will Hold Us Nicely

Come, Sweet,
from your vast continent,
to my small bed
which will hold us nicely.

Come,
from your white infinite beaches,
to stand at my window
which will frame us in sunlight.

Come,
from our memories' timeless reach,
to kiss me *again;,*
to lift our hearts in daring delight
in Heaven's twilight this side of midnight.

Spires, Signals, Sky

This poem is like a fire
for you to see atop the spires
of far away horizons.

This poem is like a mirror
sending forward Heaven's light
to your blue eternal eyes.

Watch my flame.
Catch the light.
See my signals in a dusky sky:
Signals just for Thee

This Is Our River

This is our river,
our great and serious adventure:
our Nile, our Congo,
our Amazon, our Columbia.

It will be our journey
past our pyramids,
our hearts of darkness and light,
our lost cities of gold,
our expeditions
over the mountains
in our souls.

This is our river:
our great and serious adventure
of love.

Sailing

Our bed
was the quiet bay of a secret ocean
Our pillows
the fields of dawn a soft love's potion.

We gave birth to our destiny
as your body pressed to me.
In the sanctuary of fate's rooms,
our faces shone like summer moons.

On a day full of sacred emotion
we sailed on our own private ocean.

In a dream filled with love and light
we sailed away from endless night.

The Stutterer's Kiss

Let your lips be my consonants,
your tongue the tip of my thoughts.
Let us pass my broken breath between us.

Let my throat receive your words,
so your sentences can enter my story.
Let us pass our hearts along our spines,
disguised as fingertips.

Let my belly, my lower chest
access the beginning of all your breaths.
Let us bond through brand new dreams.

Let your mouth and mine
flow like water into wine

Summer's Dance

The zenith'd sun is a memory:
all the ghosts of my youth
lie languidly
against her sumptuous body.

They rise as rounded thoughts,
and fall as lotus'd pearls
in the deep of summer's dance.

These Rooms of Yours

It's a continent
with the Amazon vast,
full of jungle, swamp and mystery;

with ancient roads
to ruined alpine Inca cities.

It is labyrinthine to my experience,
a place of imagination unimaginable.

Except for these rooms of yours:

Your kitchen
with its table brown, round
and watched over by Jesus and Mary;

Your living room with its sofa,
very white (like seashore)
and its glass dancers
shaped like clear streams
caught mid-flow;

Your bedroom
with its turned-down sheets
of my dreams
in which I am Robinson Crusoe
and you welcome me home
from my lonely journey.

Light

You are the light of my life,
my lamp through the years
as they ebb and flow.

In dreams I saw you ever-closer.
My Higher Self: infinity's mirror
catching the future and long ago

when they buried you in blankets
as I rose up through oceans blue,
seeking clouds, waiting on you.

So Many Lifetimes with You

Once we were Indians,
prairie riders
gliding across the grass;
you and I, on our horses,
traveling into even earlier lands.

These days
you come from South America,
from Brazil, filled sometimes
with homesickness
but also with delicious kisses, brave,
that send sailboats floating
on the oceans of my dreams.

Near and far,
here and there,
everywhere
I find myself with you.

Quiet Astonishment

The room is full of dawn
when I awake into it,
accompanied by explanations
of you.

In these explanations,
you are never complete
and I end up a poet
in bed with his paper and pen,
struggling to describe
your face, your lips, your words;
and my quiet astonishment
concerning this lovely world
you bring me each Sunday.

Secret House

In a forest that overlooks the river,
There is a secret house.

Let me take you there
And make it, also, a sacred house.

I Float into Sleep's River

I float into sleep's river
Bible upon my chest
imagining you there too
full length upon me
your breath by cheek and neck
my touch upon your slender back
where spine begins to end
and flesh tends to ecstasy

The Long Arc

Sleeping with you, making love,
would be like sleeping
with the Bible made woman:
– books of light, of sorrows,
of rainbows over oceans
returning to their proper places;
and islands of Solomon and Sheba.

Closeness with you:
skaters slow, then,
through practice and patience,
sweet agility.

Kisses with you:
stories that coast along,
rise and fall, swift as birds,
high as moons caught in trees;
or languid as whale shapes
moving under blue ocean light.

You visit me.
You enter my rooms.
I want you
through all your seasons,
sunlight or shadow,
all their reasons.

The long arc
through years,
through disappearances
as profound to me as those
suffered by people who turn a corner
and enter a phone booth
to make one last call.

Between the Empty and the All

You made one last call
and I loved and suffered
through every syllable
of your voice.

I didn't see you again
for 17 years,
while I moved from the house
that was to have been ours,
hauled hay,
raised a daughter; or helped.

A doorway, a chaos,
a clamour of voices and duets
I did not see
disappeared into the city.
City of other lips,
other words,
other voices;
left me a graveyard of tombstones
over each of your promises.

17 years ...
17 years!

Lord Thou has given me
such experiences:
I feel so alive,
feel such feelings,
feel so rich,
feel such a need
of Thy Wisdom,
great wisdom.

All flags flying,
I return.

This Much is True

1.

This much is true:
some days I am a broken branch
wrenched from the farm,
pained by ,
burned by
wind from a sun-hole
draining the sky
and the world behind
of every possibility.

On those days I am tired
Un-revived is the Christ within me,
He's lost beyond the horizon's edge.

I am almost lost,
the spire too distant,
the boat listing,
the thread of my life
fallen in thickets.

Some days I arise,
not tall,
feeling uncalled,
lost from my past.

Am I required from now on
to leave the wire down
on fences no longer strong
fallen in thickets?

2.

And then,
sometimes true
and shimmering there,
golden day green field flair,
is her red-tressed beauty,

On winded waves:
the sledding boats' fast float,
the ocean's blue green.

From granite cliffs:
the dangled kites stretch,
the quick bright breeze.

From camps at dusk:
cloud-mingled moon and sky,
embered stars in between.

This much is true:
some days I am a broken branch

Darker Powers

I rose with her atop the tower
where was a room
lived in by darker powers.

Where was a room
devoid of flowers
no open curtains, no daylight hours.

Devoid of flowers.
Lilacs lost to dim backwaters
where wait the snake's ghastly daughters.

I rose with her atop the tower
where was a room
lived in by darker powers.

Where was a room
ruined in shadows
from needle moons, and pale white powders.

Ruined in shadows.
She lit the candle.
With cadaverous fingers,
I was handled.

I rose with her atop the tower
where was a room
lived in by darker powers.

Fifteen Years Ago

Blue tractor under more blue sky,
fifteen years ago, the loamy soil
of the Lower Field
peeled by the silver disk
of the cutting wheel:
Time clicking past
a round shimmering clock.

I cannot refuse that feeling:
The ploughing steady and familiar,
the odd rock chiming high, in my ear,
the steering, the gearing,
history in my hands,
the diesel's deep steady roar.

Down here at the coast
I feel lost. There's a ticket tossed
in a pocket I cannot find –
a door that needs unlocking,
a mystery river unwinding, a ship's docking
at the very edge of my hearing.

At the distant end of an unknown journey
a ghost of me tramps the ancient lane,
goes by the barns, slips between the trees
to the Lower Field and, kneeling,
feels the alfalfa's green dampness,
the stalks of timothy and Kentucky blue grass,
lifts his gaze to the Selkirks in the distance
glances at the sun and then, done,
considers the scene with humble deference.

Dislocation

It's been 32 years, yet
your gravel pit death
still transects my mind's breadth
with the vastness of its effect.

Angst for years in my mother's mind,
she feeling afflicted – even Divinely;
from sloughs, swamps,
bottom-land caves
oceanic dreams of tidal waves
flooded, succeeding
fields of summers in sadness.

We were all captured, engraved
by nightmares of tractors
falling backwards over banks;
by reveries and memories of last moments
as our cosmos dislocated itself.

Let Me Be Your Lancelot

You were an underground river
seeking fields and light,
wanting to touch the sky.

Now you are
a reborn woman,
ending your long, lonely night.

So, gather the sun in your sky-blue dress
and wear the fields of green in your hat,
as you and Percival ride
along the shady forest track.

I am beside you too –
in spirit, idea and thought.

Let me be your Lancelot.

Isabelle

Isabelle
with her long snowshoe stride
comes alive
in this landscape oracular
with its ancient gods residing,
not yet gone,
just beyond the horizon.

She is the woman,
the one:
to look at Red Indian
with me,
to stand in our yard's garden
with me
in the womanhood of early autumn,
filled with dreams and auguries.

She has sailed far to arrive here;

Isabelle,
with her gentle heart beating,
beside me ...

I come alive.

I Fall to Earth

You were struggling with your suitcase
on your way to me via Paris
when a wheel broke,
tripped you up and then, you said,
"I fall to earth."

Yes, you truly have fallen to earth:
you were an angel making your way
to Heaven when you fell to earth
and found yourself beside me:

You – helping me stand
true and tall against all
problems big or small.

Your soul, my soul's friend.
You my best guarantee
against unhappy endings.

History's Untraceable Pedestrians

It was a sunless day
except above the clouds
where, untied by blue,
all that the sky contains
descends to the nearest
clear horizon –

below the clouds:
history's untraceable pedestrians
meander Neanderthal-like
within the crosswalk lines.

Sitting in the Waves Café
I see, coming now, the lady
who lost her husband a few years ago.

Now that she is alone,
does she phone the help lines?
or do angels gather at her door
(as blessed alms to the desperate poor)
in the deepest middle of her lonely nights?

www.ingramcontent.com/pod-product-compliance
Lightning Source LLC
Chambersburg PA
CBHW070306120526
44590CB00017B/2578